MW01702516

Daily Reflections for Advent 2009

DAILY REFLECTIONS FOR
advent
2009

DANIEL J. HARRINGTON, S.J.

ST. ANTHONY MESSENGER PRESS
Cincinnati, Ohio

Rescript

In accord with the *Code of Canon Law*, I hereby grant my permission to publish *Daily Reflections for Advent 2009*, by Daniel J. Harrington.

Reverend Joseph R. Binzer
Vicar General
Archdiocese of Cincinnati
Cincinnati, Ohio
April 17, 2009

The permission to publish is a declaration that a book or pamphlet is considered to be free from doctrinal or moral error. It is not implied that those who have granted the permission to publish agree with the contents, opinions or statements expressed.

ISBN 978-0-86716-918-8

Published by St. Anthony Messenger Press
28 W. Liberty St.
Cincinnati, OH 45202
www.SAMPBooks.org

Printed in the United States of America.

Printed on acid-free paper.

09 10 11 12 13 5 4 3 2 1

Introduction

This booklet presents brief reflections on the Scripture passages read at the Masses each day during Advent of 2009. In cases where the readings for a special feast (November 30, December 8 and 12) replace the Advent texts for the day, I have treated both sets of readings.

For each day I identify a theme that ties together the various biblical texts, suggest a sample prayer (often using words from the Responsorial Psalm or the Alleluia verse) and offer questions that might stimulate thought and prayer.

The method employed here is a version of *lectio divina* ("sacred reading"), a practice rooted in Christian monastic history and recently used more widely in personal and pastoral settings. It involves careful reading of a biblical text and analysis of it (What does the text say?), meditation (What does the text say to me?), prayer (What do I want to say to God on the basis of this text?) and action (What should I do in light of this text?).

My hope is that during Advent this booklet will contribute to a greater appreciation of what we celebrate on Christmas Day when we hear that "the Word became flesh and lived among us" (John 1:14).

Daniel J. Harrington, S.J.

The Two Comings of Jesus

November 29 • First Sunday of Advent

Jeremiah 33:14–16; Psalm 25:4–5, 8–9, 10, 14;
1 Thessalonians 3:12—4:2; Luke 21:25–28, 34–36

The word *Advent* means "coming, arriving, becoming present." During the Advent season we tend to focus on Jesus' first coming, at his birth in the land of Israel some two thousand years ago. However, the readings for the First Sunday of Advent also point us toward Jesus' Second Coming and the fullness of God's kingdom that this event will mark. They lead us to reflect on what is the goal and horizon of Christian hope: eternal life with God through Jesus Christ.

The reading from Jeremiah 33 looks forward to an ideal descendant of King David, one who will bring justice and security to God's people. We Christians believe that Jeremiah's hopes have been fulfilled in part through Jesus' first coming. The passage from Luke 21 lists some future signs and portents that will accompany Jesus' Second Coming (known as the "birth pangs" or "woes" of the Messiah) and urges an attitude of constant vigilance in the face of them. However, Luke insists that Jesus' Second Coming should be welcomed and celebrated rather than feared "because your redemption is drawing near." What we hope for most ardently, then, we will enjoy most fully.

In the meantime, between the two comings of Jesus, Paul exhorts us to try to abound in love and holiness and act in ways appropriate to our identity as Christians. In this way we will be prepared for the judgment that will accompany "the coming of our Lord Jesus with all his saints" (1 Thessalonians 3:13).

Pray

"Lead me in your truth, and teach me,
for you are the God of my salvation;
for you I wait all day long" (Psalm 25:5).

Reflect

What do you hope for this Advent? In what sense have Jeremiah's hopes been fulfilled in Jesus? Does talk about Jesus' Second Coming frighten you or encourage you?

• • • | • • •

The Power of God's Word

November 30 • Saint Andrew, Apostle

ROMANS 10:9–18; PSALM 19:8–10; MATTHEW 4:18–22

Today the readings for Saint Andrew the Apostle replace those of the First Monday of Advent. According to Matthew (and Mark), Andrew and his brother, Simon Peter, were the first persons called by Jesus to become his disciples. Jesus meets them in their work as fishermen in Capernaum, by the Sea of Galilee. What is amazing about this narrative is the power of Jesus' words. He says, "Follow me, and I will make you fish for people" (Matthew 4:19).

There is no indication in the text that Peter and Andrew already knew Jesus. Yet at his call they were willing to leave behind their families, friends and businesses to be with Jesus and share in his ministry of teaching and healing. How attractive and convincing the words of Jesus must have been!

While the New Testament says nothing about Andrew's activities as an apostle after Jesus' death and resurrection, a rich tradition about Andrew's exploits as a missionary and miracle worker developed in early Christian writings known as the *Acts of Andrew.* While the historical foundations of much of this material may be questionable, today's reading from Romans 10 expresses what was undoubtedly the focus of the apostle's ministry: proclaiming the Good News about Jesus and bringing people to faith in God through Jesus. Thus Andrew the apostle carried out his calling to "fish for people" and bore witness to the power of God's Word.

Pray

Lord, your Word is more precious than gold and sweeter than honey. Help me to hear it more clearly and to find more effective ways of communicating it to others. Amen.

Reflect

Have you ever had an especially powerful experience of God's Word? What effect did it have on you? How have you shared it with others?

• • • | • • •

Promise and Fulfillment

November 30 • Monday of the First Week of Advent

Isaiah 2:1–5; Psalm 122:1–9; Matthew 8:5–11

Hope is the central theme of Advent. The Scripture readings for the season invite us to stand beside the Old Testament prophets and psalmists and to enter into their hopes for

God's people. The Gospel readings suggest how in some ways these hopes were fulfilled in Jesus. The dynamic of Advent is promise and fulfillment.

The psalmist describes his pilgrimage to the temple and prays for the peace and prosperity of Jerusalem. The prophet Isaiah hopes that all nations might come to God's holy mountain in Jerusalem and be instructed in God's ways, that thus God's Word might go out to all peoples and that as a result there will be perfect peace in the world.

According to Matthew 8, Jesus fulfills some aspects of the promise-and-fulfillment dynamic sketched by Isaiah. A centurion (presumably a non-Jew) approaches Jesus (a Jew) in the hope that he might heal his servant (presumably also a non-Jew). As a military man, he knows the power of verbal commands. He goes so far as to believe that the Word of Jesus had the power to heal his servant's maladies. Thus the

Word of the Lord goes forth to Gentiles, and Jesus in turn foresees that believing non-Jews like the centurion and his servant will join the great patriarchs of Israel at the messianic banquet in God's kingdom. What Isaiah hoped for, Jesus makes into reality.

Pray

"Restore us, O God;
let your face shine, that we may be saved" (Psalm 80:3).

Reflect

What makes Isaiah's vision so powerful in imagery and content? What makes the centurion's faith so remarkable? How does Jesus fulfill the promises made in Isaiah's vision?

• • • | • • •

Beyond Their Hopes

December 1 • Tuesday of the First Week of Advent

ISAIAH 11:1–10; PSALM 72:1–2, 7–8, 12–13, 17;
LUKE 10:21–24

For much of ancient Israel's history (from about 1000 to 587 BC) there were kings ruling over God's people. With a few exceptions, however, these kings were disappointing or even worse. They failed politically, morally and religiously. One of the great hopes expressed repeatedly by Israel's prophets was for an ideal king. Today's readings from Isaiah 11 and Psalm 72 are expressions of that hope.

The ideal king was to be a descendant of David ("from the stump of Jesse"), widely regarded as the best king of all (though not without faults) (Isaiah 11:1). He was to be a wise and just leader, one who would bring about peace—to the extent that even natural enemies like wolves and lambs would live together peaceably. Through this ideal king, so the prophets hoped, all the nations would come to know and worship the God of Israel in his holy temple at Jerusalem.

Following the lead of some of Jesus' Jewish contemporaries, early Christians celebrated Jesus as the Son of David and the Messiah or Christ (the "anointed one"). In ancient Israel kings were anointed (see Psalm 2). Nevertheless, today's passage from Luke 10 reminds us that Jesus was even more than the Son of David, the Messiah or the ideal king. Rather, Jesus identifies himself as the Son of God who is both the revealer of God and the revelation of God. In this way Jesus surpassed even the greatest hopes of ancient Israel's prophets for an ideal king.

Pray

"May all nations be blessed in him;
  may they pronounce him happy"
(Psalm 72:17).

Reflect

How would you describe an ideal leader? What kind of leader did the ancient Israelite prophets want? How does Jesus differ from what those prophets sought?

• • • | • • •

The Mountain and the Meal

December 2 • Wednesday of the First Week of Advent

Isaiah 25:6–10; Psalm 23:1–6; Matthew 15:29–37

Psalm 23 ("The Lord is my shepherd") is the most famous among the 150 prayers in the book of Psalms. So beautiful and consoling is the shepherd imagery in its first half that we tend to neglect the images of the meal in verse 5 ("You prepare a table before me") and the mountain in verse 6 ("the house of the LORD") on the Temple Mount in Jerusalem as the place of God's presence in its second half.

The images of the mountain and the meal also appear in Isaiah 25. The phrase "on this mountain" occurs three times in verses 6, 7 and 10. The prophet looks forward to a rich feast for all peoples there and describes the Lord as destroying death forever and wiping away all our tears. Both Old Testament texts portray "this mountain" as the place where we may find perfect joy with God in a sumptuous meal.

The hopes associated with the mountain and the meal find some fulfillment in Jesus' actions according to Matthew 15. When Jesus ascends a mountain (presumably in Galilee), large crowds follow him and approach him, place before him many persons in need of healing and are amazed at his ability to cure them. Then, rather than sending them away hungry, the compassionate Jesus miraculously provides for the crowds an abundant meal of bread and fish, with even a large amount of leftovers. Once more, the hopes glimpsed in the Old Testament become realities in the New Testament.

Pray

"[T]his is our God; we have waited for him, so
that he might save us"
(Isaiah 25:9).

Reflect

Where do you find God especially present to you? Why are mountains so often places of religious experience in the Bible and today? How might the biblical meal imagery contribute to your appreciation of the Eucharist?

• • • | • • •

An Eternal Rock

December 3 • Thursday of the First Week of Advent

Isaiah 26:1–6; Psalm 118:1, 8–9, 19–21, 25–27; Matthew 7:21, 24–27

In whom or what do you trust? That is a question that faces every human person. Some of us trust in political leaders, our possessions and wits or our families and friends. Nevertheless, there are times in our lives when even those sources of trust are not enough. There may be occasions when our only source of stability and security is the Lord.

One biblical image of the stability and security that only God can afford is the rock. The reading from Isaiah 26:4 affirms that "in the Lord God you have an everlasting rock." We are to imagine a huge rock, one that no one could pick up or throw, one that would be difficult for enemies to ascend and attack those finding refuge there. The stability and security provided by the "everlasting rock" is far superior to what any human leader or prince can give (as Psalm 118 indicates).

Today's Gospel reading comes from the very end of Jesus' Sermon on the Mount. In Matthew 5–7, Jesus presents a summary of his wise teachings. By way of conclusion he insists that his wisdom is something to be acted upon. It is not merely philosophical speculation or memorized formulas. He goes on to appeal to the image of a house built upon a rock, on a solid foundation that can resist storms without collapsing under pressure. As Wisdom incarnate, Jesus, the wise teacher, provides the "everlasting rock" that is our best source of stability and security.

Pray

"Trust in the Lord forever,
  for in the LORD GOD
  you have an everlasting rock" (Isaiah 26:4).

Reflect

Whom or what do you rely on when you are in trouble? How do you imagine an "everlasting rock"? Do you find Jesus' Sermon on the Mount a good foundation for your life?

• • • | • • •

The Blind Shall See

December 4 • Friday of the First Week of Advent

ISAIAH 29:17–24; PSALM 27:1, 4, 13–14; MATTHEW 9:27–31

The Old Testament readings for today and tomorrow offer rays of hope in the midst of one of ancient Israel's darkest periods. They are taken from chapters 28 to 33 of the book of Isaiah and reflect a setting in the late eighth century BC when King Hezekiah of Judah rebelled against the Assyrians. The result was that Jerusalem came very close to being destroyed in 701 BC.

The prophet Isaiah opposed the rebellion, criticized the leaders and their supporters and warned about what might happen. Nevertheless, he was convinced that somehow the God of Israel would save the city from destruction. In the midst of his criticisms and warnings, Isaiah also offered hopeful visions of what life might be like when the crisis subsided. Because Isaiah trusted in God's power to reverse the situation, he presented a vision promising the restoration of nature, miraculous healings, punishment of evildoers and renewed worship in Jerusalem. One sign of the restoration of God's people would be that "out of their gloom and darkness / the eyes of the blind shall see" (29:18).

In Matthew 9, Jesus restores the sight of two blind men. Their faith in Jesus' power to heal leads Jesus to grant their request. Thus Isaiah's promise of the renewed people of God was being fulfilled in part through Jesus opening the eyes of the blind.

Pray

"The LORD is my light and my salvation;
whom shall I fear?" (Psalm 27:1).

Reflect

Why did Isaiah remain hopeful in such a dangerous situation? How does Jesus' healing the blind men suggest that his public ministry was a special time? Why does Jesus command the men to be silent, and how could they ignore his wishes?

• • • | • • •

The Teacher of Israel

December 5 • Saturday of the First Week of Advent

ISAIAH 30:19–21, 23–26; PSALM 147:1–6;
MATTHEW 9:35—10:1, 5–8

Isaiah's second vision of hope for the people of Jerusalem against the background of the crisis of 701 BC features an unusual description of God as the Teacher of Israel: "[Y]et your Teacher will not hide himself any more, but your eyes shall see your Teacher" (30:20). The divine Teacher will tell his people, "This is the way; walk in it" (30:21). Isaiah's vision of the renewed people includes the peace of Jerusalem, the land made fertile by abundant waters, the prosperity of herds and flocks and a bruised people healed by God.

One of the strong emphases in Matthew's Gospel is its portrayal of Jesus as the teacher of Israel. It features five substantial speeches by Jesus and identifies him as the "one instructor" (23:10). Today's passage serves as a summary of Jesus' teaching and healing activities, as well as an introduction to his Missionary Discourse.

Jesus teaches and heals out of compassion for his people who lack good leaders and so are like "sheep without a shepherd" (Matthew 9:36). Recognizing the need for coworkers, he commissions his twelve disciples to share in his mission of teaching and healing the people of God. They are to do what he did—preach about God's kingdom and bring healing to those in need of it. They are to minister to "the lost sheep of the house of Israel" (Matthew 10:6). Only after Jesus' death and resurrection will their mission expand to all nations (Matthew 28:19). Thus the Teacher of Israel becomes the Teacher of the world.

Pray

"Great is our Lord, and abundant in power;
his understanding is beyond measure"
(Psalm 147:5).

Reflect

Why did Israel in Isaiah's time need God as its teacher? How does the prophet's vision point forward to Jesus' proclamation of God's kingdom? What does Matthew's description of Jesus as the "one instructor" suggest about Jesus' divinity?

• • • | • • •

The Shape of Hope

December 6 • Second Sunday of Advent

Baruch 5:1–9; Psalm 126:1–6;
Philippians 1:4–6, 8–11; Luke 3:1–6

Hope involves looking forward to something desirable in the expectation that it may become a reality. In the Bible God is the origin, ground and goal of hope. Today's Old Testament passages view Israel's return from exile in Babylon in the sixth century BC from three perspectives. The quotation from Isaiah 40 in Luke 3 reflects the beginning of the return. In Baruch 5 Jerusalem is personified as a woman witnessing the exiles' return. Psalm 126 indicates that Israel's hope had become a reality and reflects on the joy that the people felt. The origin of this hope was the God who created them, chose them and promised to be with them always. The ground was what God had done for this people in the exodus from Egypt. The goal of this hope was the renewal of the worship of God in the Holy City and the resumption of life as a nation again.

The biblical dynamic of hope did not stop in the sixth century BC. Today's New Testament readings show that while God remains the origin and ground of our hope, the goal has become even bigger and better. According to Luke, John the Baptist prepared the way for Jesus as the way by which "all flesh shall see the salvation of God" (3:6). And Paul prays that the good work begun by God when the Philippian Christians accepted the Good News about Jesus might lead them to be found "pure and blameless" for the day of Christ, that is, at his Second Coming and the last judgment (Philippians 1:10).

Pray

"The LORD has done great things for us,
 and we rejoiced" (Psalm 126:3).

Reflect

How do you understand the shape of hope? Why was ancient Israel's return from exile such a major event? How can you best prepare for fullness of life with Jesus in God's kingdom?

• • • | • • •

New Beginnings

December 7 • Monday of the Second Week of Advent

Isaiah 35:1–10; Psalm 85:9–14; Luke 5:17–26

The return from exile in Babylon in the sixth century BC marked a new beginning in ancient Israel's history. Today's reading from Isaiah 35 captures the hope and excitement of the journey home, along with some of the fear that often accompanies new beginnings. The prophet first portrays the desert between Babylon and Jerusalem as coming to life with all kinds of beautiful flowers and trees. Then he encourages the fearful among the travelers by identifying God as their leader and guide and promises miraculous healings along the way. Finally he pictures the road home as pleasant, fertile, safe from dangerous animals and issuing in a joyous arrival.

Today's Gospel reading from Luke 5 features another kind of new beginning—for a lame man, thus fulfilling one of the prophecies of Isaiah 35, "[T]hen the lame shall leap like a deer" (v. 6). In his new beginning the lame man is supported by friends who go to extraordinary means to bring him to Jesus because they believed in Jesus' power to heal even a paralyzed person. They got even more than they hoped for. When Jesus saw their faith, he not only healed the man's lameness but also declared that his sins were forgiven. Thus Jesus made possible a new beginning for this lame man on both the physical and spiritual levels. Although some objected to Jesus declaring anyone's sins forgiven, the crowd as a whole glorified God for making these new beginnings possible.

Pray

"Be strong, do not fear!
Here is your God.
He will come with vengeance,
with terrible recompense.
He will come and save you" (Isaiah 35:4).

Reflect

Imagine yourself as one of the travelers described in Isaiah 35—what do you see, and how do you feel? Are there any new beginnings for you at this time of year? What do you hope for, and what frightens you?

• • • | • • •

Mary Is Different

December 8 • The Immaculate Conception of the Blessed Virgin Mary

GENESIS 3:9–15, 20; PSALM 98:1–4;
EPHESIANS 1:3–6, 11–12; LUKE 1:26–38

The narrative of the "fall" or the "original sin" in Genesis 3 explains why there is sin and death in the world, why we all seem to repeat the experience of Adam and Eve and why we all suffer the disastrous consequences of their (and our) disobedience with regard to God's command. According to the doctrine of the Immaculate Conception, Mary was conceived without original sin and so was divinely prepared to be the mother of Jesus, the Son of God. That makes her different from us.

What makes Mary different from the rest of us comes out especially in the angel Gabriel's greeting to Mary according to Luke: "Greetings, favored one! The Lord is with you!" (1:28). Thus Mary is designated as the special object of divine favor ("favored one") and so is deemed worthy to bear the child conceived by the Holy Spirit, the child called the Son of God. This is how Mary differs from you and me.

Today's selection from the Letter to the Ephesians comes from the opening benediction, which reflects on the effects or benefits of Jesus' life, death and resurrection for all who are "in Christ": election, holiness, divine favor and so on. In a sense, Mary, free from original sin, experienced these benefits even before the birth of her son. Having been freed from the dominion of sin and death through Christ, now we too can enjoy those benefits, and so we can be like Mary.

Pray

Holy Mary, Mother of God, pray for us sinners, now and at the hour of our death. Amen.

Reflect

Do you see evidence of "original sin" in yourself and those around you? Do you approach God through Mary in prayer? Read Ephesians 1:3–14 with reference first to Mary and then to yourself.

• • • | • • •

The Good Shepherd

December 8 • Tuesday of the Second Week of Advent

ISAIAH 40:1–11; PSALM 96:1–3, 10–13; MATTHEW 18:12–14

The book of Isaiah is the major source of Old Testament readings during Advent. From the perspective of literary beauty and theological depth, the second part of that book, chapters 40 through 55, represents the high point of the Old Testament. It was composed around 537 BC, in response to the Persian King Cyrus's permission for the Judean exiles in Babylon to return home and rebuild Jerusalem and its temple.

Today's reading from Isaiah 40 introduces a collection of prophetic discourses and hymns. Its scene is the heavenly court or council. There, God decrees an end to Israel's punishment for its sins, and another voice declares that the people's return will be a triumphant procession with God in the lead. Toward the end of the passage God is pictured as a shepherd leading, protecting and nurturing his flock. In the ancient Near East kings were often portrayed as shepherds, and the beloved Psalm 23 ("the LORD is my shepherd") applies the image to the God of Israel. The return from exile will be proof of God's care and fidelity for his lost people, and so it deserves a "new song" (Psalm 96:1).

In Matthew 18, Jesus uses the image of the shepherd to describe his own concern (and that of his Father) for those who stray. While the imagery shifts from the exile community to individuals, it serves the same purpose: to emphasize God's concern for the lost and God's eagerness to find and restore them to himself.

Pray

"Sing to the LORD, bless his name;
 tell of his salvation from day to day"
(Psalm 96:2).

Reflect

Why might the exiles in Babylon have felt lost? Why was it appropriate in the ancient Near East to portray kings and God as shepherds? Does Jesus' parable of the Good Shepherd console you?

• • • | • • •

Rest for the Weary

December 9 • Wednesday of the Second Week of Advent

ISAIAH 40:25–31; PSALM 103:1–4, 8, 10;
MATTHEW 11:28–30

Not every Israelite in Babylon in the sixth century BC eagerly responded to the prophet's call to return to Jerusalem. Some were convinced that God had given up on them while others found themselves exhausted and hopeless after fifty years of exile. The prophet whom we call Second Isaiah had to use all his rhetorical skills and persuasive powers to convince his fellow exiles to join him on the journey home.

The beautiful poem in Isaiah 40 portrays the God of Israel as the ultimate source of power and energy for exhausted and hopeless people. The first part reminds the exiles that their God is the ideal leader for the journey home yet one who knows each follower by name. The second part reassures them that God will supply the energy that the people will need for their difficult trip. The key is their hope and trust in the Lord's ability to lead them on (despite all the obstacles) toward the "rest" they will find in their ancestral home.

In what sounds like an invitation to Jesus' school in Matthew, Jesus the teacher promises "rest" to exhausted persons, those who "are weary and are carrying heavy burdens" (11:28). A yoke is a harness placed on beasts of burden who might power a plow or a mill. Jesus claims that his yoke is easy and his burden is light. He is an ideal teacher, not arrogant or excessively demanding but instead "gentle and humble in heart" (Matthew 11:29).

Pray

"Bless the LORD, O my soul,
and do not forget all his benefits"
(Psalm 103:2).

Reflect

Do you find prayer energizing? Does hope empower you to do necessary and important things even when you are tired? What did your best teachers do to make learning both productive and easy?

• • • | • • •

Small Hopes and Big Hopes

December 10 • Thursday of Second Week of Advent

ISAIAH 41:13–20; PSALM 145:1, 9–13; MATTHEW 11:11–15

In the Old Testament, prophets speak on God's behalf. They convey God's Word to God's people. While they often look to the future, they also frequently refer to the past (creation, exodus, Israel's sins, etc.) and the present (especially current political and religious crises).

They offer criticisms and warnings as well as words of consolation and hope.

The hope of the prophet whom we call Second Isaiah was concrete and well focused. He was trying to convince the Judean exiles in sixth century BC Babylon to return to Jerusalem and renew God's people there. Today's passage from Isaiah 41 seeks to reassure the people that their God will lead them home safely and soundly. In the face of difficult terrain, God promises to make things easy (like a knife cutting hot butter). In the face of fear about traveling through the desert, God promises to supply abundant water (to drink) and vegetation (for shade). In the end all will understand that the Lord's hand has made the return possible and successful.

Six centuries later God raised up John the Baptist as a prophet. In his dress and lifestyle, John evoked memories of Elijah. He, too, criticized and warned God's people while pointing toward the full coming of God's kingdom. John's hopes were much more universal and even cosmic than those of Second Isaiah. We Christians believe that John's hopes began to be fulfilled in Jesus' public ministry as we continue to pray, "Thy kingdom come."

Pray

"Your kingdom is an everlasting kingdom,
and your dominion endures throughout all generations" (Psalm 145:13).

Reflect

What do you understand the term "prophet" to mean? How do Second Isaiah's prophecies look some twenty-five hundred years later? How do they prepare for the prophecies of John the Baptist and Jesus?

• • • | • • •

The Wise Prophet

December 11 • Friday of the Second Week of Advent

Isaiah 48:17–19; Psalm 1:1–4, 6; Matthew 11:16–19

Prophets are seldom popular. They often tell truths that people do not want to hear. As a result, they suffer verbal and even physical abuse. Both John the Baptist and Jesus suffered and were executed for telling hard truths.

Today's passage from Matthew 11 provides a sample of the verbal abuse that these two prophets of God's kingdom endured. Because John adopted a rigorously ascetic lifestyle, it was said "He has a demon" (Matthew 11:18). Because Jesus used meals with all kinds of persons as vehicles for symbolizing and anticipating what life in God's kingdom will be like, he was criticized as a glutton and a drunkard and branded as a friend of tax collectors and sinners.

In the face of these criticisms, Jesus contends that "wisdom is vindicated by her deeds" (Matthew 11:19). The meaning of this saying is illuminated by today's Old Testament readings. In Isaiah 48, God identifies himself as Israel's redeemer and holy one, pleads with his people to follow his wise commandments and promises them prosperity for many generations if they follow God's way. Psalm 1 contrasts the way of the wise and righteous with the way of the foolish and wicked. We all have to make a choice about which way we will take. For Christians, Jesus shows the correct way. He is not only a wise teacher but also Wisdom incarnate. And he proves the authenticity of his wisdom by what he does.

Pray

Lord God, Heavenly Father, may I accept the challenges of Jesus your prophet and put into practice his wise teachings. Amen.

Reflect

How are prophets treated today? Which way have you chosen in your life—wisdom or folly? How do you try to practice the wisdom of Jesus?

• • • | • • •

A Woman Clothed With the Sun

December 12 • Our Lady of Guadalupe

ZECHARIAH 2:10–13 (OR REVELATION 11:19; 12:1–6, 10); JUDITH 13:18–19; LUKE 1:26–38

The Feast of Our Lady of Guadalupe stems from an apparition of the Blessed Virgin Mary to a Mexican peasant named Juan Diego in the sixteenth century. It has been celebrated in Mexico for many years and now increasingly in the United States, to the extent that its readings supersede those of the day of Advent on which it falls.

The Old Testament reading from Zechariah helps us appreciate Mary as "daughter Zion" (2:10) thus situating her in Israel as the historic people of God. The optional passage from Revelation fits the apparition even better, especially with its expression "a woman clothed with the sun" (Revelation 12:1). The woman is clearly the Mother of the Messiah. She is also a symbol of the people of God and the church. The various descriptions of the woman can enrich our appreciation of Mary as the Mother of the church. While a glorious figure, she is also persecuted by the "great red dragon" (Satan) and must flee to a place prepared for her by God (Revelation 12:3).

The cosmic significance of Mary in the book of Revelation is balanced by the very human reaction she exhibits in Luke 1 when she is commissioned to be the mother of the Son of God. At first she appears confused and hesitant. However, when reassured that her child will be from the Holy Spirit, she responds positively with words that make her a major Advent figure, "Here am I, the servant of the Lord; let it be with me according to your word" (1:38).

Pray

Blessed are you, holy Virgin Mary, deserving of all praise; from you arose the sun of justice, Christ our God.

Reflect

What does it mean to call Mary the "Mother of the church"? Can you identify with Mary's confusion and hesitancy? Why is Mary a key Advent figure?

• • • | • • •

Elijah and John the Baptist

December 12 • Saturday of the Second Week of Advent

SIRACH 48:1–4, 9–11; PSALM 80:2–3, 15–19;
MATTHEW 17:10–13

The prophet Elijah is a major character in 1 and 2 Kings. Elijah and his successor Elisha were active in the ninth century BC, and the stories about them are among the most fascinating and attractive parts of the Old Testament. According to 2 Kings 2, Elijah was taken up to heaven in a fiery whirlwind. In some circles it was believed that Elijah would return to earth "before the great and terrible day of the LORD" (Malachi 4:5).

In the second century BC, a Jewish wisdom teacher named Jesus son of Eleazar son of Sirach produced a summary of the great figures of biblical history up to his own time. Today's Old Testament reading is part of his section on Elijah. It presents Elijah as a reflection of the glory of God and gives special attention to his ascension into heaven and alludes to his role before the day of the Lord.

The dialogue between Jesus and his disciples after his Transfiguration concerns Elijah and his return. The Transfiguration of Jesus on a mountain in Galilee is a preview of the fullness of God's kingdom. The disciples were puzzled because in their view Elijah had not yet returned to prepare the day of the Lord. In response Jesus suggests that Elijah had already come in the person of John the Baptist. At the same time he forecasts that the fate that befell John will happen to him too.

Pray

"Turn again, O God of hosts;
look down from heaven, and see"
(Psalm 80:14).

Reflect

Why did Jesus identify John as Elijah? In what sense is Elijah an Advent figure? Do you regard saints as reflections of God's glory?

• • • | • • •

Rejoice in the Lord!

December 13 • Third Sunday of Advent

ZEPHANIAH 3:14–18; ISAIAH 12:2–6; PHILIPPIANS 4:4–7; LUKE 3:10–18

The Third Sunday of Advent is known as "Gaudete Sunday," from one of the Latin words for "rejoice" (*gaudere*). The title comes from the first word in today's reading from Paul's Letter to the Philippians, "Rejoice in the Lord always." Joy is an emotion evoked by good fortune, success or well being. According to the Bible, God is the origin and object of true joy. Today's Old Testament readings from Zephaniah 3 and Isaiah 12 proclaim that the real reason for joy is their experience of God's presence in the midst of God's people.

Today's New Testament readings connect joy with the two comings (or advents) of Jesus. In Luke John the Baptist points toward Jesus' coming on the public stage as the "more powerful" (3:16) one who will bring baptism with the Holy Spirit and inaugurate a new phase in the full coming of God's kingdom. In Philippians Paul urges joy at the first coming of

Jesus and points forward with joy to his Second Coming ("the Lord is near") (4:5).

To be productive, joy needs direction and follow-through, if it is not to pass as fast as it came. Thus John the Baptist urges various groups to make concrete their joy at the coming of God's kingdom by sharing their possessions with others and treating people fairly and honestly. Likewise, Paul exhorts the Philippians to thank and pray to God and so find peace and confidence in God as they await the fullness of God's kingdom.

Pray

"Rejoice in the Lord always; again I will say, Rejoice. Let your gentleness be known to everyone. The Lord is near" (Philippians 4:4–5).

Reflect

What makes you happy? How do you translate your joy into action? Do you find joy in the Lord?

• • • | • • •

The Prophet's Authority

December 14 • Monday of the Third Week of Advent

NUMBERS 24:2–7, 15–17; PSALM 25:4–9;
MATTHEW 21:23–27

In the Bible a true prophet speaks for God. That is, the prophet communicates to God's people the Word of God. The veracity of the prophet can be judged by the results of the prophecy—does it come to pass or not?

Today's reading from Numbers features a very unusual prophet. Balaam son of Beor was not an Israelite. He was hired by Balak the king of Moab to prophesy against Israel. He was supposed to be a propagandist in the service of Israel's enemy. But instead of prophesying Israel's destruction, Balaam conveyed a vision of Israel's victory and prosperity. Moreover, Balaam foresaw the rise of a great leader in Israel, "[A] star shall come out of Jacob, and a scepter shall rise out of Israel" (24:17). Despite himself, Balaam speaks God's Word and offers consolation and encouragement on Israel's behalf. As Christians we believe that his prophecy of the star has been fulfilled in Jesus (see the Magi episode in Matthew 2:1–12).

Today's passage from Matthew 21 concerns the origin of the authority of John the Baptist and Jesus as prophets. In response to a question about his own authority, Jesus shifts the discussion to John's authority: Was it of heavenly or of human origin? His question poses a dilemma for the opponents, and so they refuse to answer. However, it is clear from the incident that Jesus believed that John's authority and his own authority came from God and that they were true prophets as they spoke God's Word to God's people.

Pray

"Lead me in your truth, and teach me,
for you are the God of my salvation"
(Psalm 25:5).

Reflect

How could God use the pagan Balaam as a true prophet? What does it mean to describe John and Jesus as true prophets? What do such prophets do?

• • • | • • •

The Lowly and Humble Remnant

December 15 • Tuesday of the Third Week of Advent

ZEPHANIAH 3:1–2, 9–13; PSALM 34:2–3, 6–7, 17–19, 23; MATTHEW 21:28–32

A remnant is something left over from something larger. Several of the Old Testament prophets hoped for a remnant within Israel that would faithfully carry on its identity and tradition as God's people and restore and renew Israel's religious life.

In the seventh century BC the prophet Zephaniah hoped for such a remnant in Judah. In the first part of today's selection from chapter 3, the prophet warns the people of Jerusalem about the dire consequences of their failure to trust and obey God. Nevertheless, he foresees "that day" (3:11) on which all peoples will call upon the name of the Lord and there will be within Israel as a remnant "a people humble and lowly" (3:12). This remnant will carry on Israel's life with justice and truthfulness and live in peace and prosperity.

The remnant within Israel that responded positively to John the Baptist and Jesus were for the most part "a people humble and lowly." Both had greatest success among marginal persons such as tax collectors and sinners. The chief priests and elders were puzzled at that, and the parable of the two sons tries to explain it. While marginal persons initially refused God's call to repent, they did so eventually and so became part of the remnant. On the contrary, the religious leaders first showed interest in John and Jesus but failed to follow up. Thus

Zephaniah's prophecy of a humble and lowly remnant was being fulfilled in John and Jesus.

Pray

"My soul makes its boast in the LORD;
let the humble hear and be glad"
(Psalm 34:2).

Reflect

Does the idea of a "humble and lowly" remnant surprise you? What is the point of Jesus' parable of the two sons? With what persons does the church today have the best success in its missionary efforts?

• • • | • • •

The One God and His Messiah

December 16 • Wednesday of the Third Week of Advent

ISAIAH 45:6–8, 18, 21–25; PSALM 85:9–14; LUKE 7:18–23

Judaism, Christianity and Islam are distinctive for their belief in only one God. The clearest and most definitive statement of biblical monotheism appears in today's reading from Isaiah 45. Part of Second Isaiah, this text is surprising in that its historical setting was one of ancient Israel's darkest hours—exile in Babylon.

In this passage the God of Israel claims to be the one and only God, the creator of heaven and earth and the Lord of all. He asserts, "I am the LORD, and there is no other"(45:6). He affirms that only in him are just deeds and power possible. And he promises to be the vindication and glory of his people Israel. The one and only God is the God of Israel.

While insisting on Jewish monotheism, the early Christians celebrated Jesus as the Son of God and applied titles and concepts proper to the one God. It is also surprising that Jews, like most early Christians, could so easily call upon him as "the Lord Jesus Christ" soon after his resurrection. This phenomenon is better described as an explosion than a development of doctrine.

What encouraged this explosion is captured in today's reading from Luke 7. In response to emissaries from John the Baptist, Jesus affirms that he has done the "works" of the Messiah: "the blind receive their sight, the lame walk, the lepers are cleansed, the deaf hear, the dead are raised, the poor have good news brought to them" (7:22). In other words, Jesus does what only God can do.

Pray

"[L]et the earth open, that salvation may spring up; and let it cause righteousness to sprout up also" (Isaiah 45:8).

Reflect

How do you understand God's claim to "make weal and create woe"? (Isaiah 45:7). What does it mean to call Jesus "the one who is to come"? (Luke 7:19). How do you balance the humanity and divinity of Jesus?

• • • | • • •

Who is Jesus? Part One

December 17 • Thursday of the Third Week of Advent

GENESIS 49:2, 8–10; PSALM 72:1–4, 7–8, 17;
MATTHEW 1:1–17

Beginning with the readings of December 17, the Advent Gospel readings lead up to the birth of Jesus celebrated on Christmas Day. The two selections from Matthew 1 read today and tomorrow answer the question: Who is Jesus? They situate Jesus in the context of ancient Israel's history and how he fulfills the Jewish Scriptures.

The genealogy of Jesus in Matthew 1:1–17 identifies Jesus as the son of Abraham and the son of David, thus linking him to two great biblical figures. The list of Jesus' ancestors is divided into three sections, each with fourteen generations and introduced by Abraham, David and the exile generation. The men included in the first two sections are a mix of saints and sinners, while we know nothing about those listed between Zerubbabel and Joseph. This neat and orderly sequence is interrupted by mentions of four women—Tamar, Rahab, Ruth and Bathsheba—whose unusual ancestry or actions somehow prepared for the highly unusual birth of Jesus from the Virgin Mary. All this diversity goes into the birth of "Jesus the Messiah" (1:1).

The reading from Genesis 49 is part of Jacob's farewell discourse to his twelve sons. The section about Judah has been chosen because Jesus and David belonged to the royal tribe of Judah. Psalm 72 is a prayer for the king, which was very likely composed for and sung at the coronations of kings in Judah. All these texts root Jesus firmly within Israel's history while preparing for his surprising exploits on behalf of God's marvelously diverse people.

Pray

O Wisdom of our God Most High, guiding creation with power and love: Come to teach us the path of knowledge!

Reflect

How does Matthew's genealogy of Jesus serve as a fitting introduction to the New Testament? What contribution does the inclusion of the women make in the genealogy? How do today's readings help in answering the question: Who is Jesus?

• • • | • • •

Who Is Jesus? Part Two

December 18 • Friday of the Third Week of Advent

JEREMIAH 23:5–8; PSALM 72:1–2, 12–13, 18–19; MATTHEW 1:18–25

Though often regarded as a prophet of doom, Jeremiah was also a prophet of hope. In today's excerpt he looks forward to "a righteous Branch" of David (a just king) and return from exile

(23:5). We Christians believe that Jeremiah's prophecies have been fulfilled in Jesus.

The second part of Matthew 1 continues answering the question: Who is Jesus? It first explains how Jesus, the Son of God, conceived in Mary by the Holy Spirit, became the Son of David when Joseph accepted the legal paternity of Mary's child. Thus as a human being, Jesus became the object of the promises and prophecies associated with Israel's most famous king and his descendants.

According to Matthew 1, Joseph gave his legal son the name *Jesus*, which is a form of Joshua and means "the Lord saves." In many cultures a child is given a name that signifies what the parents hope the child will become. Jesus grew up to become the Savior of the world.

In fulfilling Isaiah 7:14 ("[T]he young woman is with child and shall bear a son…"), Jesus also gained the title "Emmanuel" or "God is with us" (Matthew 1:23). He is the presence of

God among humankind. Just as Matthew's Gospel begins by identifying Jesus as "God is with us," so it ends with the Risen Jesus' promise to be with his disciples always.

Pray

O Leader of the House of Israel, giver of the Law to Moses on Sinai: Come to rescue us with your mighty power!

Reflect

What does it mean that Jesus is both Son of David and Son of God? In what sense does Jesus as an adult live up to his name? How is he Emmanuel in your life?

• • • | • • •

Birth Announcements

December 19 • Saturday of the Third Week of Advent

JUDGES 13:2–7, 24–25; PSALM 71:3–6, 16–17; LUKE 1:5–25

Luke's Infancy Narrative begins with announcements of the births of John and Jesus. In these texts, John appears as great, but Jesus is even greater. The reading from Judges 13 concerns the announcement of Samson's birth, and it prepares for the angel's proclamation that John "must never drink wine or strong drink" (Luke 1:15). Likewise, the psalmist's profession in Psalm 71:6 ("Upon you I have leaned from my birth; it was you who took me from my mother's womb") prepares for Gabriel's prophecy that John would be filled with the Holy Spirit "even before his birth" (Luke 1:15).

The story of John and Jesus begins at the Jerusalem temple. John's parents, Zechariah and Elizabeth, represent the best in Jewish piety. They were in Jerusalem so that Zechariah could perform his annual priestly duty. The announcement of John's birth takes place while Zechariah is burning incense and the people are at prayer. The angel Gabriel appears to Zechariah and proclaims that his son will be like Elijah and will prepare God's people for the coming of the Lord. When he raises doubts, the angel gives him the sign that he will be unable to speak until all this happens. (For the announcement of Jesus' birth in Luke 1:26–38, see my comments for December 8 and 12.) While there are common features in the two birth announcements, the major difference is that Mary's child will be the Son of the Most High, and his kingdom will have no end. John is great, but Jesus is even greater.

Pray

O Root of Jesse's stem, sign of God's love for all his people: Come to save us without delay!

Reflect

In what ways do Zechariah and Elizabeth exemplify the best in Jewish piety? Can you sympathize with Zechariah's hesitation? What roles will John play as an adult?

• • • | • • •

God's Fidelity to Us

December 20 • Fourth Sunday of Advent

MICAH 5:1–4; PSALM 80:2–3, 15–16, 18–19;
HEBREWS 10:5–10; LUKE 1:39–45

Fidelity involves trust in someone and belief in something. Many people today find it very hard to be faithful to anyone or anything. Those who live in a moral and religious vacuum cannot be faithful. Those who live only for the moment cannot remain faithful.

The biblical concept of fidelity has as its object and central concern God and God's Word. From that basic fidelity there should flow fidelity in all the aspects of our lives. Fidelity involves living out the grand narrative contained in Scripture (the story of our salvation) and being part of its great living tradition (the church throughout the centuries). The Bible presents us with many examples of God's fidelity to his people and of men and women among God's people who have proved themselves faithful to God.

Today's Old Testament reading from Micah (a contemporary of Isaiah) contains God's promise of a descendant of David who would be born in the area of Bethlehem, who would shepherd his people even better than David did and whose greatness would reach to the ends of the earth. Psalm 80 echoes the promise of a shepherd king like David and prays that God will be with "the one at your right hand" (80:17). We Christians believe that these promises have been fulfilled in Jesus. Because God is faithful to us as his people, we can and should be faithful to God and to one another.

Pray

O Key of David, opening the gates of God's eternal kingdom: Come and free the prisoners of darkness!

Reflect

To whom and to what do you try to be faithful? Have there been times when you have not been faithful? Why is standing in the biblical tradition important as a basis for fidelity?

• • • | • • •

Mary as Faithful to God's Word

December 21 • Monday of the Fourth Week of Advent

Songs of Songs 2:8–14 (or Zephaniah 3:14–18); Psalm 33:2–3, 11–12, 20–21; Luke 1:39–45

Perhaps originally a human love song, the Song of Songs has long been interpreted by both Jews and Christians as a symbolic representation of God's loving fidelity toward his people. Today's reading from Luke's Gospel is the same as yesterday's. It describes the Visitation of Mary (the prospective mother of Jesus) to Elizabeth (the prospective mother of John the Baptist). Luke is fond of personal examples, and he portrays Mary as a model of loving fidelity to God and God's Word.

Though much older and the wife of a priest, Elizabeth acknowledged the superior status of Mary's son and of Mary herself by referring to Mary as "the mother of my Lord" (the title given to the queen mother at the royal court) (Luke 1:43). She goes on to characterize Mary's greatness in terms of her fidelity to God and God's Word: "And blessed is she who believed that there would be a fulfillment of what was spoken to her by the Lord" (1:45). The basis for Mary's fidelity was God's Word delivered through the angel Gabriel that she would become the mother of the Son of the Most High. Mary trusted that the God of Israel would make it possible for her to carry out her commission and, through her Son, be a pivotal instrument in God's plan for a new and better relationship with humankind. Mary was faithful to someone (God) and to something (God's Word). For that kind of fidelity she was and is rightly called "blessed."

Pray

O Emmanuel, our King and Giver of Law: Come to save us, Lord our God!

Reflect

Can you name an example of extraordinary fidelity that you have experienced? What has enabled you to be faithful in your life? Do you ever ask Mary for help in remaining faithful?

• • • | • • •

Mary's Song

December 22 • Tuesday of the Fourth Week of Advent

1 Samuel 1:24–28; 1 Samuel 2:1, 4–8; Luke 1:46–56

Mary's song in response to Elizabeth's blessing of her is known as the *Magnificat,* from the first word in the Latin translation. In it Mary praises God for choosing her to be the "mother of my Lord" (Luke 1:43).

The Old Testament background of Mary's song is the account of Samuel's birth. In 1 Samuel 1 and 2, we learn that God blesses the barren Hannah with a boy, and she in turn dedicates him to the Lord at the sanctuary in Shiloh. Samuel will grow up to become a great leader in Israel. Then Hannah breaks into song in celebration of what God had done for her and her people. Mary's song contains many echoes of Hannah's song in 1 Samuel 2, especially with regard to how God shows special care for the poor and lowly.

In Mary's song she first praises God for allowing her, despite the "lowliness of his servant," to bring the Son of the Most High into the world and foresees that her son will affect many generations to come (Luke 1:48). Then she describes the surprising ways of God in scattering the proud, casting down the mighty, lifting up the lowly, satisfying the hungry and sending the rich away empty. Finally she relates what God was doing through her to how God was fulfilling his promises to Abraham and his descendants. Thus Mary's song places Jesus in the wider context of salvation history and helps us understand better the God who is revealed in the Bible.

Pray

O Radiant Dawn, splendor of eternal light, sun of justice: Come and shine on those who dwell in darkness and in the shadow of death!

Reflect

What similarities do you find between Hannah's song and Mary's song? What do their songs contribute to your understanding of God? In what sense is Jesus' birth part of God's "great reversal"?

• • • | • • •

What Will This Child Be?

December 23 • Wednesday of the Fourth Week of Advent

MALACHI 3:1–4, 4:5–6; PSALM 25:4–5, 8–9, 10, 14; LUKE 1:57–66

Luke's accounts of the births of John and Jesus continue the comparison begun with the announcements of their births. They suggest that while John is great, Jesus is even greater.

Today's Old Testament reading from Malachi 3 describes God sending a messenger to prepare the way for the Lord's coming and promising that Elijah will return before "the great and terrible day of the LORD"(Malachi 4:5). In his ministry of baptism in the face of the coming kingdom of God, John prepared the way for Jesus and fulfilled Malachi's prophecy about the divine messenger and Elijah.

John's birth to his aged parents was correctly interpreted as a display of God's mercy. The name *John* can be traced to the Hebrew name *Yochanan*, which means "the Lord has shown mercy." Thus the name fits the person and his role in salvation history. With the child's naming, Zechariah's muteness is lifted, and he proclaims the hymn known as the *Benedictus* (tomorrow's reading).

What will this child be? The neighbors' question receives an answer as Luke's narrative proceeds. John will grow up to be a preacher of repentance and the one who prepares for Jesus' public ministry. He will serve as the divine messenger and the prophet like Elijah. As in their births, so in their public ministries, John will be great but Jesus will be even greater.

Pray

O King of all nations and keystone of the church: Come and save humankind which you formed from the dust!

Reflect

In what sense was John's birth a display of God's mercy? How might John serve as a model for all Christians? How do you relate the two comings of Jesus?

• • • | • • •

Zechariah's Song

December 24 • Thursday of the Fourth Week of Advent

2 Samuel 7:1–5, 8–12, 14, 16; Psalm 89:2–5, 27, 29:
Luke 1:67–79

Throughout Advent a major theme has been promise and fulfillment. To use Augustine's formula, what lies hidden in the Old Testament becomes clear in the New.

Today's Old Testament reading is from Nathan's prophecy to David in 2 Samuel 7. There, God reminds David that he chose David and made him a powerful king and promises to protect him from his enemies and establish an everlasting dynasty: "Your house and your kingdom shall be made sure forever before me; your throne shall be established forever" (7:16). However, as 2 Kings makes clear, the house of David was destroyed by the Babylonians in the early sixth century BC.

Early Christians believed that God's promises to David were fulfilled through his descendant Jesus. Zechariah's song known as the *Benedictus* (from the first word of the Latin translation) places Jesus' birth in the context of God's promise to raise up a mighty savior from the house of David. It celebrates Jesus in terms of God's mercy and covenant fidelity, God's promise to Abraham of freedom to worship God without fear and the new possibility of holiness and right relationship with God. Only near the end does Zechariah mention John's ministry as a prophet preparing the way for the advent of the Davidic Messiah. Once again, while John is great, Jesus is even greater.

Pray

O Radiant Dawn, splendor of eternal light, sun of justice: Come and shine on those who dwell in darkness and in the shadow of death.

Reflect

How do you interpret the absence of conditions or stipulations in God's covenant with David? How does Zechariah's song reinforce the greatness of Jesus? Where does his son, John, fit in salvation history?

• • • | • • •

What Does Christmas Really Mean?

December 25 • The Nativity of the Lord

ISAIAH 52:7–10; PSALM 98:1–6; HEBREWS 1:1–6; JOHN 1:1–18

The readings for the Masses celebrated on Christmas Day are concerned more with indicating the significance of Jesus' birth than with supplying the details surrounding the event.

The Old Testament passage from Isaiah 52 celebrates the return of God's people from exile and the restoration of Jerusalem as God's dwelling place. As was the case throughout Advent, the reading situates Jesus in relation to God's special people Israel. Psalm 98 is a "new song" (98:1) one that is appropriate to the new manifestation of God's saving power in the birth of Jesus. Here the emphasis is on Jesus' significance for "all the ends of the earth" (98:3).

The reading from John celebrates Jesus as the "Word" of God (1:1). In Jesus, God has spoken. In him God has revealed to us what God most eagerly wanted to communicate to us. Jesus' identity as both the revealer and the revelation of God is the key to understanding John's Gospel and indeed the entire New Testament. Jesus' role as the Word of God and the Wisdom of God is affirmed also in today's passage from Hebrews. There he is described in terms like those used in the book of Wisdom: "the reflection of God's glory and the exact imprint of God's very being" (Hebrews 1:3). The whole of the Advent season leads up to the proclamation made in John 1:14: "And the Word became flesh and lived among us, and we have seen his glory, the glory as of the father's only son, full of grace and truth."

Pray

Come, you nations, and adore the Lord. For today a great light has come upon the earth.

Reflect

How do today's readings balance Jesus' roots in Israel and his universal significance? Why is the title "the Word of God" so important? In what sense is Jesus the Wisdom of God?